THE VOICE OF THE MASTER

KAHLIL GIBRAN

The Voice
of the Master

translated from the Arabic by
ANTHONY R. FERRIS

A Citadel Press Book
Published by Carol Publishing Group

Carol Publishing Group Edition - 1992

A Citadel Press Book
Published by Carol Publishing Group
Citadel Press is a registered trademark of Carol Communications, Inc.

Editorial Offices: 600 Madison Avenue, New York, NY 10022
Sales & Distribution Offices: 120 Enterprise Avenue, Secaucus, NJ 07094
In Canada: Canadian Manda Group, P.O. Box 920, Station U, Toronto,
Ontario, M8Z 5P9, Canada

Queries regarding rights and permissions should be addressed to:
Carol Publishing Group, 600 Madison Avenue, New York, NY 10022

Manufactured in the United States of America
ISBN 0-8065-0022-0

25 24 23 22 21 20 19 18 17 16 15 14

I came to say a word and I shall say it now. But if death prevents me, it will be said by Tomorrow, for Tomorrow never leaves a secret in the book of Eternity.

I came to live in the glory of Love and the light of Beauty, which are the reflections of God. I am here, living, and I cannot be exiled from the domain of life, for through my living word I will live in death.

I came here to be for all and with all, and what I do today in my solitude will be echoed Tomorrow by the multitude.

What I say now with one heart will be said Tomorrow by thousands of hearts.

Kahlil Gibran

CONTENTS

CONTENTS

THE VOICE OF THE MASTER

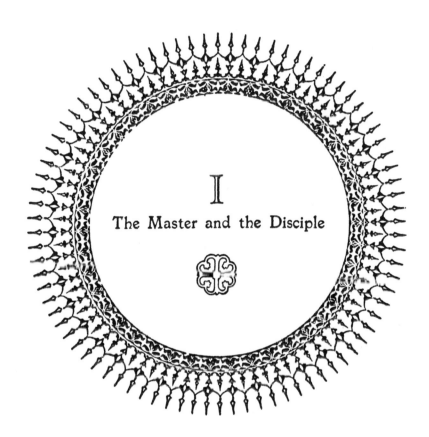

I

The Master and the Disciple

I

The Master's Journey to Venice

AND IT CAME TO PASS that the Disciple saw the Master walking silently to and fro in the garden, and signs of deep sorrow showed upon his pale face. The Disciple greeted the Master in the name of Allah, and inquired after the cause of his grief. The Master motioned with his staff, and bade the Disciple seat himself on the rock by the fish pond. The Disciple did so, and made ready to listen to the Master's story.

Said the Master:

"You desire me to tell you of the tragedy which Memory reenacts every day and night upon the stage of my heart. You are weary of my long silence and my unspoken secret, and you are troubled by my sighs and lamentations. To yourself you say, 'If the Master will not admit me into the temple of his sorrows, how shall I ever enter into the house of his affections?'

"Hearken to my story . . . Listen, but do not pity me;

13

for pity is intended for the weak—and I am still strong in my affliction.

"From the days of my youth, I have been haunted, waking and sleeping, by the phantom of a strange woman. I see her when I am alone at night, sitting by my bedside. In the midnight silence I hear her heavenly voice. Often, when I close my eyes, I feel the touch of her gentle fingers upon my lips; and when I open my eyes, I am overcome with dread, and suddenly begin listening intently to the whispered sounds of Nothingness. . . .

"Often I wonder, saying to myself, 'Is it my fancy that sets me spinning until I seem to lose myself in the clouds? Have I fashioned from the sinews of my dreams a new divinity with a melodious voice and a gentle touch? Have I lost my senses, and in my madness have I created this dearly loved companion? Have I withdrawn myself from the society of men and the clamor of the city so that I might be alone with the object of my adoration? Have I shut my eyes and ears to Life's forms and accents so that I might the better see her and hear her divine voice?'

"Often I wonder: 'Am I a madman who is content to be alone, and from the phantoms of his loneliness fashions a companion and spouse for his soul?'

"I speak of a *Spouse*, and you marvel at that word. But how often are we puzzled by some strange experience, which we reject as impossible, but whose reality we cannot efface from our minds, try as we will?

"This visionary woman has indeed been my spouse,

14

sharing with me all the joys and sorrows of life. When I awake in the morning, I see her bending over my pillow, gazing at me with eyes glowing with kindness and maternal love. She is with me when I plan some undertaking, and she helps me bring it to fulfilment. When I sit down to my repast, she sits with me, and we exchange thoughts and words. In the evening, she is with me again, saying, 'We have tarried too long in this place. Let us walk in the fields and meadows.' Then I leave my work, and follow her into the fields, and we sit on a high rock and gaze at the distant horizon. She points to the golden cloud; and makes me aware of the song the birds sing before they retire for the night, thanking the Lord for the gift of freedom and peace.

"Many a time she comes to my room when I am anxious and troubled. But no sooner do I spy her, than all care and worry are turned to joy and calm. When my spirit rebels against man's injustice to man, and I see her face amidst those other faces I would flee from, the tempest in my heart subsides and is replaced by the heavenly voice of peace. When I am alone, and the bitter darts of life stab at my heart, and I am chained to the earth by life's shackles, I behold my companion gazing at me with love in her eyes, and sorrow turns to joy, and Life seems an Eden of happiness.

"You may ask, how can I be content with such a strange existence, and how can a man, like myself, in the spring-time of life, find joy in phantoms and dreams? But I say to you, the years I have spent in this state are the cornerstone of

15

all that I have come to know about Life, Beauty, Happiness, and Peace.

"For the companion of my imagination and I have been like thoughts freely hovering before the face of the sun, or floating on the surface of the waters, singing a song in the moonlight—a song of peace that soothes the spirit and leads it toward ineffable beauty.

"Life is that which we see and experience through the spirit; but the world around us we come to know through our understanding and reason. And such knowledge brings us great joy or sorrow. It was sorrow I was destined to experience before I reached the age of thirty. Would that I had died before I attained the years that drained my heart's blood and my life's sap, and left me a withered tree with branches that no longer move in the frolicsome breeze, and where birds no longer build their nests."

The Master paused, and then, seating himself by his Disciple, continued:

"Twenty years ago, the Governor of Mount Lebanon sent me to Venice on a scholarly mission, with a letter of recommendation to the Mayor of the city, whom he had met in Constantinople. I left Lebanon on an Italian vessel in the month of Nisan. The spring air was fragrant, and the white clouds hung above the horizon like so many lovely paintings. How shall I describe to you the exultation I felt during the journey? Words are too poor and too scant to express the inmost feeling in the heart of man.

"The years I spent with my ethereal companion were filled with contentment, joy, and peace. I never suspected

16

that Pain lay in wait for me, or that Bitterness lurked at the bottom of my cup of Joy.

"As the carriage bore me away from my native hills and valleys, and toward the coast, my companion sat by my side. She was with me during the three joyful days I spent in Beirut, roaming the city with me, stopping where I stopped, smiling when a friend accosted me.

"When I sat on the balcony of the inn, overlooking the city, she joined me in my reveries.

"But when I was about to embark, a great change swept over me. I felt a strange hand seizing hold of me and pulling me back; and I heard a voice within me whispering, 'Turn back! Do not go! Turn back to the shore before the ship sets sail!'

"I did not heed that voice. But when the ship hoisted sail, I felt like a tiny bird that had suddenly been snatched between the claws of a hawk and was being borne aloft into the sky.

"In the evening, as the mountains and hills of Lebanon receded on the horizon, I found myself alone at the prow of the ship. I looked around for the woman of my dreams, the woman my heart loved, the spouse of my days, but she was no longer at my side. The beautiful maiden whose face I saw whenever I gazed at the sky, whose voice I heard in the stillness of the night, whose hand I held whenever I walked the streets of Beirut—was no longer with me.

"For the first time in my life I found myself utterly alone on a boat sailing the deep ocean. I paced the deck, calling to her in my heart, gazing on the waves in the hope

17

of seeing her face. But all in vain. At midnight, when all the other passengers had retired, I remained on deck, alone, troubled, and anxious.

"Suddenly I looked up, and I saw her, the companion of my life, above me, in a cloud, a short distance from the prow. I leaped with joy, opened my arms wide, and cried out, 'Why have you forsaken me, my beloved! Where have you gone? Where have you been? Be near me now, and never leave me alone again!'

"She did not move. On her face I descried signs of sorrow and pain, something I had never seen before. Speaking softly and in sad tones she said, 'I have come from the depths of the ocean to see you once more. Now go down to your cabin, and give yourself over to sleep and dreams.'

"And having uttered these words, she became one with the clouds, and vanished. Like a hungry child I called to her frantically. I opened my arms in all directions, but all they embraced was the night air, heavy with dew.

"I went down to my berth, feeling within me the ebb and flow of the raging elements. It was as if I were on another boat altogether, being tossed on the rough seas of Bewilderment and Despair.

"Strangely enough, as soon as I touched my pillow, I fell fast asleep.

"I dreamt, and in my dream I saw an apple tree shaped like a cross, and hanging from it, as if crucified, was the companion of my life. Drops of blood fell from her hands and feet upon the falling blossoms of the tree.

18

"The ship sailed on, day and night, but I was as though lost in a trance, not certain whether I was a human being sailing to a distant clime or a ghost moving across a cloudy sky. In vain I implored Providence for the sound of her voice, or a glimpse of her shadow, or the soft touch of her fingers on my lips.

"Fourteen days passed and I was still alone. On the fifteenth day, at noon, we sighted the coast of Italy at a distance, and at dusk we entered the harbor. A throng of people in gaily decorated gondolas came to greet the ship and convey the passengers to the city.

"The City of Venice is situated on many small islands, close to one another. Its streets are canals and its numerous palaces and residences are built on water. Gondolas are the only means of transportation.

"My gondolier asked where I was going, and when I told him to the Mayor of Venice, he looked at me with awe. As we moved through the canals, night was spreading her black cloak over the city. Lights gleamed from the open windows of palaces and churches, and their reflection in the water gave the city the appearance of something seen in a poet's dream, at once charming and enchanting.

"When the gondola reached the junction of two canals, I suddenly heard the mournful ringing of church bells. Though I was in a spiritual trance, and far removed from all reality, the sounds penetrated my heart and depressed my spirits.

"The gondola docked, and tied up at the foot of marble

steps that led to a paved street. The gondolier pointed to a magnificent palace set in the middle of a garden and said: 'Here is your destination.' Slowly I climbed the steps leading to the palace, followed by the gondolier carrying my belongings. When I reached the gate, I paid him and dismissed him with my thanks.

"I rang, and the door was opened. As I entered I was greeted by sounds of wailing and weeping. I was startled and amazed. An elderly servant came toward me, and in a sorrowful voice asked what was my pleasure. 'Is this the palace of the Mayor?' I inquired. He bowed and nodded, and I handed him the missive given me by the Governor of Lebanon. He looked at it and solemnly walked toward the door leading to the reception room.

"I turned to a young servant and asked the cause of the sorrow that pervaded the room. He said that the Mayor's daughter had died that day, and as he spoke, he covered his face and wept bitterly.

"Imagine the feelings of a man who has crossed an ocean, all the while hovering between hope and despair, and at the end of his journey stands at the gate of a palace inhabited by the cruel phantoms of grief and lamentation. Imagine the feelings of a stranger seeking entertainment and hospitality in a palace, only to find himself welcomed by white-winged Death.

"Soon the old servant returned, and bowing, said, 'The Mayor awaits you.'

"He led me to a door at the extreme end of a corridor, and motioned to me to enter. In the reception room I found

20

a throng of priests and other dignitaries, all sunk in deep silence. In the center of the room, I was greeted by an elderly man with a long white beard, who shook my hand and said, 'It is our unhappy lot to welcome you, who come from a distant land, on a day that finds us bereft of our dearest daughter. Yet I trust our bereavement will not interfere with your mission, which, rest assured, I shall do all in my power to advance.'

"I thanked him for his kindness and expressed my deepest grief. Whereupon he led me to a seat, and I joined the rest of the silent throng.

"As I gazed at the sorrowful faces of the mourners, and listened to their painful sighs, I felt my heart contracting with grief and misery.

"Soon one after the other of the mourners took his departure, and only the grief-stricken father and I remained. When I, too, made a movement to leave, he held me back, and said, 'I beg you, my friend, do not go. Be our guest, if you can bear with us in our sorrow.'

"His words touched me deeply, and I bowed in acquiescence, and he continued, 'You men of Lebanon are most open-handed toward the stranger in your land. We should be seriously remiss in our duties were we to be less kind and courteous to our guest from Lebanon.' He rang, and in response to his summons a chamberlain appeared, attired in a magnificent uniform.

" 'Show our guest to the room in the east wing,' he said, and take good care of him while he is with us.'

21

"The chamberlain conducted me to a spacious and lav-
ishly appointed room. As soon as he was gone, I sank down
on the couch, and began reflecting on my situation in this
foreign land. I reviewed the first few hours I had spent
here, so far away from the land of my birth.

"Within a few minutes, the chamberlain returned, bring-
ing my supper on a silver tray. After I had eaten, I began
pacing the room, stopping now and then at the window
to look out upon the Venetian sky, and to listen to the
shouts, of the gondoliers and the rhythmic beat of their
oars. Before long I became drowsy, and dropping my
wearied body on the bed, I gave myself over to an oblivion,
in which was mingled the intoxication of sleep and the
sobriety of wakefulness.

"I do not know how many hours I spent in this state,
for there are vast spaces of life which the spirit traverses,
and which we are unable to measure with time, the inven-
tion of man. All that I felt then, and feel now, is the
wretched condition in which I found myself.

"Suddenly I became aware of a phantom hovering above
me, of some ethereal spirit calling to me, but without any
sensible signs. I stood up, and made my way toward the hall,
as though prompted and drawn by some divine force. I
walked, will-less, as if in a dream, feeling as though I
were journeying in a world that was beyond time and space.

"When I reached the end of the hall, I threw open a
door and found myself in a vast chamber, in the center of
which stood a coffin surrounded by flickering candles and

wreaths of white flowers. I knelt by the side of the bier and looked upon the departed. There before me, veiled by death, was the face of my beloved, my life-long companion. It was the woman I worshipped, now cold in death, white-shrouded, surrounded by white flowers, and guarded by the silence of the ages.

"O Lord of Love, of Life, and of Death! Thou art the creator of our souls. Thou leadest our spirits toward light and darkness. Thou calmest our hearts and makest them to quicken with hope and pain. Now Thou hast shown me the companion of my youth in this cold and lifeless form.

"Lord, Thou hast plucked me from my land and hast placed me in another, and revealed to me the power of Death over Life, and of Sorrow over Joy. Thou hast planted a white lily in the desert of my broken heart, and hast removed me to a distant valley to show me a withered one.

"Oh friends of my loneliness and exile: God has willed that I must drink the bitter cup of life. His will be done. We are naught but frail atoms in the heaven of the infinite; and we cannot but obey and surrender to the will of Providence.

"If we love, our love is neither from us, nor is it for us. If we rejoice, our joy is not in us, but in Life itself. If we suffer, our pain lies not in our wounds, but in the very heart of Nature.

"I do not complain, as I tell this tale; for he who complains doubts Life, and I am a firm believer. I believe in the worth of the bitterness mingled in each potion that I drink from the cup of Life. I believe in the beauty of the sorrow that penetrates my heart. I believe in the ultimate mercy of these steel fingers that crush my soul.

"This is my story. How can I end it, when in truth it has no ending?

"I remained on my knees before that coffin, lost in silence, and I stared at that angelic face until dawn came. Then I stood up and returned to my room, bowed under the heavy weight of Eternity, and sustained by the pain of suffering humanity.

"Three weeks later I left Venice and returned to Lebanon. It was as though I had spent aeons of years in the vast and silent depths of the past.

"But the vision remained. Though I had found her again only in death, in me she was still alive. In her shadow I have labored and learned. What those labors were, you, my disciple, know well.

"The knowledge and wisdom I have acquired I strove to bring to my people and their rulers. I brought to Al-Haris, Governor of Lebanon, the cry of the oppressed, who were being crushed under the injustices and evils of his State and Church officials.

"I counseled him to follow the path of his forefathers and to treat his subjects as they had done, with clemency, charity, and understanding. And I said to him, 'The people are the glory of our kingdom and the source of its wealth.' And I said further, 'There are four things a ruler should banish from his realm: Wrath, Avarice, Falsehood, and Violence.'

"For this and other teachings I was chastised, sent into exile, and excommunicated by the Church.

"There came a night when Al-Haris, troubled in heart, was unable to sleep. Standing at his window, he contemplated the firmament. Such marvels! So many heavenly bodies lost in the infinite! Who created this mysterious and admirable world? Who directs these stars in their courses? What relation have these distant planets to ours? Who am I and why am I here? All these things Al-Haris said to himself.

"Then he remembered my banishment and repented of the harsh treatment he had meted out to me. At once he sent for me, imploring my pardon. He honored me with an official robe and proclaimed me before all the people as his advisor, placing a golden key in my hand.

"For my years in exile I regret nothing. He who would seek Truth and proclaim it to mankind is bound to suffer. My sorrows have taught me to understand the sorrows of my fellow men; neither persecution nor exile have dimmed the vision within me.

"And now I am tired . . ."

Having finished his story, the Master dismissed his Disciple, whose name was Almuhtada, which means "the Convert," and went up to his retreat to rest body and soul from the fatigues of ancient memories.

2

The Death of the Master

Two weeks later, the Master fell ill, and a multitude of admirers came to the hermitage to inquire after his health. When they reached the gate of the garden, they saw coming out of the Master's quarters a priest, a nun, a doctor, and Almuhtada. The beloved Disciple announced the death of the Master. The crowd began to wail and lament, but Almuhtada neither wept nor spoke a word.

For a time the Disciple pondered within himself, then he stood upon the rock by the fish pond, and spoke:

"Brothers and countrymen: You have just heard the news of the Master's death. The immortal Prophet of Lebanon has given himself over to eternal sleep, and his blessed soul is hovering over us in the heavens of the spirit, high beyond all sorrow and mourning. His soul has cast off the servitude of the body and the fever and burdens of this earthly life.

"The Master has left this world of matter, attired in the garments of glory, and has gone to another world free of hardships and afflictions. He is now where our eyes cannot see him and our ears cannot hear him. He dwells in the world of the spirit, whose inhabitants sorely need him. He is now gathering knowledge in a new cosmos, whose history and beauty have always fascinated him and whose speech he has always striven to learn.

"His life on this earth was one long chain of great deeds. It was a life of constant thought; for the Master knew no rest except in work. He loved work, which he defined as *Visible Love.*

"His was a thirsty soul that could not rest except in the lap of wakefulness. His was a loving heart that overflowed with kindness and zeal.

"Such was the life he led on this earth. . . .

"He was a spring of knowledge that issued from the bosom of Eternity, a pure stream of wisdom that waters and refreshes the mind of Man.

"And now that river has reached the shores of Eternal Life. Let no intruder lament for him or shed tears at his departure!

"Remember, only those who have stood before the Temple of Life, and never fructified the earth with one drop of the sweat of their brow are deserving your tears and lamentations when they leave it.

"But as for the Master—did he not spend all the days of his life laboring for the benefit of Mankind? Is there any among you who has not drunk from the pure fountain of his wisdom? And so, if you wish to honor him, offer his blessed soul a hymn of praise and thanksgiving, and not your mournful dirges and laments. If you wish to pay him due reverence, assert your claim to a portion of the knowledge in the books of wisdom he has left as a legacy to the world.

"Do not *give* to genius, but *take* from him! Thus only shall you be honoring him. Do not mourn for him, but be merry, and drink deeply of his wisdom. Only thus will you be paying him the tribute rightly his."

After hearing the words of the Disciple, the multitude returned to their homes, with smiles upon their lips, and songs of thanksgiving in their hearts.

Almuhtada was left alone in this world; but loneliness never possessed his heart, for the voice of the Master always resounded in his ears, urging him to carry on his work and sow the words of the Prophet in the hearts and minds of all who would listen of their own free will. He spent many hours alone in the garden meditating upon the scrolls which the Master had bequeathed to him, and in which he had set down his words of wisdom.

After forty days of meditation, Almuhtada left his Master's retreat and began his wanderings through the hamlets, villages, and cities of Ancient Phoenicia.

One day, as he was crossing the market place of the city of Beirut, a multitude followed him. He stopped at a public walk, and the throng gathered around him, and he spoke to them with the voice of the Master, saying:

"The tree of my heart is heavy with fruit; come, ye hungry ones, and gather it. Eat and be satisfied. . . . Come and receive from the bounty of my heart and lighten my burden. My soul is weary under the weight of gold and silver. Come, ye seekers after hidden treasures, fill your purses and relieve me of my burden. . . .

"My heart overflows with the wine of the ages. Come, all ye thirsty ones, drink and quench your thirst.

"The other day I saw a rich man standing at the temple door, stretching out his hands, which were full of precious stones, toward all passers-by, and calling to them, saying: 'Have pity on me. Take these jewels from me. For they have made my soul sick and hardened my heart. Pity me, take them, and make me whole again.'

"But none of the passers-by paid heed to his pleas.

"And I looked at the man, and I said to myself, 'Surely it were better for him to be a pauper, roaming the streets of Beirut, stretching out a trembling hand for alms, and returning home at eventide empty-handed.'

"I have seen a wealthy and open-handed sheik of Damascus, pitching his tents in the wilderness of the Arabian desert, and by the sides of the mountains. In the evening he sent his slaves out to waylay travelers and bring them to his tents to be sheltered and entertained. But the rough roads were deserted, and the servants brought him no guests.

"And I pondered the plight of the lonely sheik, and my

29

heart spoke to me, saying: 'Surely it is better for him to be a straggler, with a staff in his hand and an empty bucket hanging from his arm, sharing at noontide the bread of friendship with his companions by the refuse heaps at the edge of the city. . . .'

"In Lebanon I saw the Governor's daughter rising from her slumber, attired in a precious gown. Her hair was sprinkled with musk and her body was anointed with perfume. She walked into the garden of her father's palace, seeking a lover. The dewdrops upon the carpeted grass moistened the hem of her garment. But alas! Among all her father's subjects there was no one who loved her.

"As I meditated upon the wretched state of the Governor's daughter, my soul admonished me, saying, 'Were it not better for her to be the daughter of a simple peasant, leading her father's flocks to pasture and bringing them back to the fold in the evening, with the fragrance of the earth and of the vineyards in her coarse shepherd's gown? At the very least, she could steal away from her father's hut, and in the silence of the night walk toward her beloved, waiting for her by the murmuring brook!'

"The tree of my heart is heavy with fruit. Come, ye hungry souls, gather it, eat and be satisfied. My spirit overflows with aged wine. Come, oh ye thirsty hearts, drink and quench your thirst. . . .

"Would that I were a tree that neither blossoms nor bears fruit; for the pain of fertility is harsher than the bitterness of barrenness; and the ache of the open-handed rich is more terrible than the misery of the wretched poor. . . .

"Would that I were a dry well, so people might throw stones into my depths. For it is better to be an empty well than a spring of pure water untouched by thirsty lips.

"Would I were a broken reed, trampled by the foot of man, for that is better than to be a lyre in the house of one whose fingers are blistered and whose household is deaf to sound.

"Hear me, Oh ye sons and daughters of my motherland; meditate upon these words that come to you through the voice of the Prophet. Make room for them in the precincts of your heart, and let wisdom's seed blossom in the garden of your soul. For that is the precious gift of the Lord."

And the fame of Almuhtada spread all over the land, and many people came to him from other countries to do him reverence and to listen to the spokesman of the Master.

Physicians, men-of-law, poets, philosophers overwhelmed him with questions whenever they would meet him, whether in the street, in the church, in the mosque, or in the synagogue, or any other place where men foregather. Their minds were enriched by his beautiful words, which passed from lips to lips.

He spoke to them of Life and the Reality of Life, saying:

"Man is like the foam of the sea, that floats upon the

31

surface of the water. When the wind blows, it vanishes, as if it had never been. Thus are our lives blown away by Death. . . .

"The Reality of Life is Life itself, whose beginning is not in the womb, and whose ending is not in the grave. For the years that pass are raught but a moment in eternal life; and the world of matter and all in it is but a dream compared to the awakening which we call the terror of Death.

"The ether carries every sound of laughter, every sigh that comes from our hearts, and preserves their echo, which responds to every kiss whose source is joy.

"The angels keep count of every tear shed by Sorrow; and they bring to the ears of the spirits hovering in the heavens of the Infinite each song of Joy wrought from our affections.

"There, in the world to come, we shall see and feel all the vibrations of our feelings and the motions of our hearts. We shall understand the meaning of the divinity within us, whom we contemn because we are prompted by Despair.

"That deed which in our guilt we today call weakness, will appear tomorrow as an essential link in the complete chain of Man.

"The cruel tasks for which we received no reward will live with us, and show forth in splendor, and declare our glory; and the hardships we have sustained shall be as a wreath of laurel on our honored heads . . ."

Having uttered these words, the Disciple was about to withdraw from the crowds and repose his body from the labors of the day, when he spied a young man gazing at a lovely girl, with eyes that reflected bewilderment.

And the Disciple addressed him, saying:

"Are you troubled by the many faiths that Mankind professes? Are you lost in the valley of conflicting beliefs? Do you think that the freedom of heresy is less burdensome than the yoke of submission, and the liberty of dissent safer than the stronghold of acquiescence?

"If such be the case, then make Beauty your religion, and worship her as your godhead; for she is the visible, manifest and perfect handiwork of God. Cast off those who have toyed with godliness as if it were a sham, joining together greed and arrogance; but believe instead in the divinity of beauty that is at once the beginning of your worship of Life, and the source of your hunger for Happiness.

"Do penance before Beauty, and atone for your sins, for Beauty brings your heart closer to the throne of woman, who is the mirror of your affections and the teacher of your heart in the ways of Nature, which is your life's home."

And before dismissing the assembled throng, he added:

"In this world there are two sorts of men: the men of yesterday and the men of tomorrow. To which of these do you belong, my brethren? Come, let me gaze at you, and learn whether you are of those entering into the world

33

of light, or of those going forth into the land of darkness. Come, tell me who you are and what you are.

"Are you a politician who says to himself: 'I will use my country for my own benefit'? If so, you are naught but a parasite living on the flesh of others. Or are you a devoted patriot, who whispers into the ear of his inner self: 'I love to serve my country as a faithful servant.' If so, you are an oasis in the desert, ready to quench the thirst of the wayfarer.

"Or are you a merchant, drawing advantage from the needs of the people, engrossing goods so as to resell them at an exorbitant price? If so, you are a reprobate; and it matters naught whether your home is a palace or a prison.

"Or are you an honest man, who enables farmer and weaver to exchange their products, who mediates between buyer and seller, and through his just ways profits both himself and others?

"If so, you are a righteous man; and it matters not whether you are praised or blamed.

"Are you a leader of religion, who weaves out of the simplicity of the faithful a scarlet robe for his body; and of their kindness a golden crown for his head; and while living on Satan's plenty, spews forth his hatred of Satan? If so, you are a heretic; and it matters not that you fast all day and pray all night.

"Or are you the faithful one who finds in the goodness of people a groundwork for the betterment of the whole nation; and in whose soul is the ladder of perfection leading to the Holy Spirit? If you are such, you are like a lily in the garden of Truth; and it matters not if your fragrance is lost upon men, or dispersed into the air, where it will be eternally preserved.

"Or are you a journalist who sells his principles in the markets of slaves and who fattens on gossip and misfortune and crime? If so, you are like a ravenous vulture preying upon rotting carrion.

"Or are you a teacher standing upon the raised stage of history, who, inspired by the glories of the past, preaches to mankind and acts as he preaches? If so, you are a restorative to ailing humanity and a balm for the wounded heart.

"Are you a governor looking down on those you govern, never stirring abroad except to rifle their pockets or to exploit them for your own profit? If so, you are like tares upon the threshing floor of the nation.

"Are you a devoted servant who loves the people and is ever watchful over their welfare, and zealous for their success? If so, you are as a blessing in the granaries of the land.

"Or are you a husband who regards the wrongs he has committed as lawful, but those of his wife as unlawful? If so, you are like those extinct savages who lived in caves and covered their nakedness with hides.

"Or are you a faithful companion, whose wife is ever at his side, sharing his every thought, rapture, and victory? If so, you are as one who at dawn walks at the head of a nation toward the high noon of justice, reason and wisdom.

35

"Are you a writer who holds his head high above the crowd, while his brain is deep in the abyss of the past, that is filled with the tatters and useless cast-offs of the ages? If so, you are like a stagnant pool of water.

"Or are you the keen thinker, who scrutinizes his inner self, discarding that which is useless, outworn and evil, but preserving that which is useful and good? If so, you are as manna to the hungry, and as cool, clear water to the thirsty.

"Are you a poet full of noise and empty sounds? If so, you are like one of those mountebanks that make us laugh when they are weeping, and make us weep, when they laugh.

"Or are you one of those gifted souls in whose hands God has placed a viol to soothe the spirit with heavenly music, and bring his fellow men close to Life and the Beauty of Life? If so, you are a torch to light us on our way, a sweet longing in our hearts, and a revelation of the divine in our dreams.

"Thus is mankind divided into two long columns, one composed of the aged and bent, who support themselves on crooked staves, and as they walk on the path of Life, they pant as if they were climbing toward a mountaintop, while they are actually descending into the abyss.

"And the second column is composed of youth, running as with winged feet, singing as if their throats were strung with silver strings, and climbing toward the mountaintop as though drawn by some irresistible, magic power.

"In which of these two processions do you belong, my brethren? Ask yourselves this question, when you are alone in the silence of the night.

"Judge for yourselves whether you belong with the Slaves of Yesterday or the Free Men of Tomorrow."

And Almuhtada returned to his retreat, and kept himself in seclusion for many months, while he read and pondered the words of wisdom the Master had set down in the scrolls bequeathed to him. He learned much; but there were many things he found he had not learned, nor ever heard from the lips of the Master. He vowed that he would not leave the hermitage until he had thoroughly studied and mastered all that the Master had left behind, so that he might deliver it to his countrymen. In this way Almuhtada became engrossed in the perusal of his Master's words, oblivious of himself and all around him, and forgetting all those who had hearkened to him in the market places and streets of Beirut.

In vain his admirers tried to reach him, having become concerned about him. Even when the Governor of Mount Lebanon summoned him with a request that he address the officials of the state, he declined, saying, "I shall come back to you soon, with a special message for all the people."

The Governor decreed that on the day Almuhtada was to appear all citizens should receive and welcome him with honor in their homes, and in the churches, mosques, synagogues, and houses of learning, and they should hearken with reverence to his words, for his was the voice of the Prophet.

The day when Almuhtada finally emerged from his retreat to begin his mission became a day of rejoicing and festivity for all. Almuhtada spoke freely and without hindrance; he preached the gospel of love and brotherhood. No one dared threaten him with exile from the country or excommunication from the Church. How unlike the fate of his Master, whose portion had been banishment and excommunication, before eventual pardon and recall!

Almuhtada's words were heard all over Lebanon. Later they were printed in a book, in the form of epistles, and distributed in Ancient Phoenicia and other Arabic lands. Some of the epistles are in the Master's own words; others were culled by Master and Disciple from ancient books of wisdom and lore.

II

The Words of the Master

I

Of Life

LIFE IS AN ISLAND in an ocean of loneliness, an island whose rocks are hopes, whose trees are dreams, whose flowers are solitude, and whose brooks are thirst.

Your life, my fellow men, is an island separated from all other islands and regions. No matter how many are the ships that leave your shores for other climes, no matter how many are the fleets that touch your coast, you remain a solitary island, suffering the pangs of loneliness and yearning for happiness. You are unknown to your fellow men and far removed from their sympathy and understanding.

My brother, I have seen you sitting on your hillock of gold rejoicing over your riches—proud of your treasures and secure in your belief that each handful of gold you have amassed is an invisible link that joins other men's desires and thoughts with yours.

I have seen you in my mind's eye as a great conqueror

leading your troops, intent on the destruction of your enemies' strongholds. But when I looked again, I saw naught but a solitary heart pining behind your coffers of gold, a thirsty bird in a golden cage, with its water tray empty.

I have seen you, my brother, sitting upon the throne of glory, and around you stood your people acclaiming your majesty, and singing praises of your great deeds, extolling your wisdom, and gazing upon you as though in the presence of a prophet, their spirits exulting even to the canopy of heaven.

And as you gazed upon your subjects, I saw in your face the marks of happiness and power and triumph, as if you were the soul of their body.

But when I looked again, behold I found you alone in your loneliness, standing by the side of your throne, an exile stretching his hand in every direction, as if pleading for mercy and kindness from invisible ghosts—begging for shelter, even such as has naught in it but warmth and friendliness.

I have seen you, my brother, enamoured of a beautiful woman, laying down your heart at the altar of her loveliness. When I saw her gazing upon you with tenderness and maternal love, I said to myself, "Long live Love that has done away with this man's loneliness and joined his heart with another's."

Yet, when I looked again, I saw within your loving heart another solitary heart, crying out in vain to reveal

42

its secrets to a woman; and behind your love-filled soul, another lonely soul that was like a wandering cloud, wishing in vain that it might turn into teardrops in the eyes of your beloved. . . .

Your life, my brother, is a solitary habitation separated from other men's dwellings. It is a house into whose interior no neighbor's gaze can penetrate. If it were plunged into darkness, your neighbor's lamp could not illumine it. If it were emptied of provisions, the stores of your neighbors could not fill it. If it stood in a desert, you could not move it into other men's gardens, tilled and planted by other hands. If it stood on a mountaintop, you could not bring it down into the valley trod by other men's feet.

Your spirit's life, my brother, is encompassed by loneliness, and were it not for that loneliness and solitude, you would not be *you*, nor would I be *I*. Were it not for this loneliness and solitude, I would come to believe on hearing your voice that it was my voice speaking; or seeing your face, that it was myself looking into a mirror.

2

Of the Martyrs to Man's Law

ARE YOU ONE who was born in the cradle of sorrow, and reared in the lap of misfortune and in the house of oppression? Are you eating a dry crust, moistened with tears? Are you drinking the turbid water in which are mingled blood and tears?

Are you a soldier compelled by the harsh law of man to forsake wife and children, and go forth into the field of battle for the sake of *Greed*, which your leaders mis-call *Duty?*

Are you a poet content with your crumbs of life, happy in the possession of parchment and ink, and sojourning in your land as a stranger, unknown to your fellow men?

Are you a prisoner, pent up in a dark dungeon for some petty offence and condemned by those who seek to reform man by corrupting him?

Are you a young woman on whom God has bestowed

beauty, but who has fallen prey to the base lust of the rich, who deceived you and bought your body but not your heart, and abandoned you to misery and distress?

If you are one of these, you are a martyr to man's law. You are wretched, and your wretchedness is the fruit of the iniquity of the strong and the injustice of the tyrant, the brutality of the rich, and the selfishness of the lewd and the covetous.

Comfort ye, my beloved weak ones, for there is a Great Power behind and beyond this world of Matter, a Power that is all Justice, Mercy, Pity and Love.

You are like a flower that grows in the shade; the gentle breeze comes and bears your seed into the sunlight, where you will live again in beauty.

You are like the bare tree bowed with winter's snow; Spring shall come and spread her garments of green over you; and Truth shall rend the veil of tears that hides your laughter. I take you unto me, my afflicted brothers, I love you, and I contemn your oppressors.

3

Thoughts and Meditations

LIFE TAKES US UP and bears us from one place to another; Fate moves us from one point to another. And we, caught up between these twain, hear dreadful voices and see only that which stands as a hindrance and obstacle in our path.

Beauty reveals herself to us as she sits on the throne of glory; but we approach her in the name of Lust, snatch off her crown of purity, and pollute her garment with our evil-doing.

Love passes by us, robed in meekness; but we flee from her in fear, or hide in the darkness; or else pursue her, to do evil in her name.

Even the wisest among us bows under the heavy weight

of Love; but in truth she is as light as the frolicsome breeze of Lebanon.

Freedom bids us to her table where we may partake of her savory food and rich wine; but when we sit down at her board, we eat ravenously and glut ourselves.

Nature reaches out to us with welcoming arms, and bids us enjoy her beauty; but we dread her silence and rush into the crowded cities, there to huddle like sheep fleeing from a ferocious wolf.

Truth calls to us, drawn by the innocent laughter of a child, or the kiss of a loved one; but we close the doors of affection in her face and deal with her as with an enemy

The human heart cries out for help; the human soul implores us for deliverance; but we do not heed their cries, for we neither hear nor understand. But the man who hears and understands we call mad, and flee from him.

Thus the nights pass, and we live in unawareness; and the days greet us and embrace us. But we live in constant dread of day and night.

We cling to the earth, while the gate of the Heart of the Lord stands wide open. We trample upon the bread of Life, while hunger gnaws at our hearts. How good is Life to Man; yet how far removed is Man from Life!

4

Of the First Look

IT IS THAT MOMENT that divides the intoxication of Life from the awakening. It is the first flame that lights up the inner domain of the heart. It is the first magic note plucked on the silver string of the heart. It is that brief moment that unfolds before the soul the chronicles of time, and reveals to the eyes the deeds of the night, and the works of conscience. It opens Eternity's secrets of the future. It is the seed cast by Ishtar, goddess of Love, and sown by the eyes of the beloved in the field of Love, brought forth by affection, and reaped by the Soul.

The first glance from the eyes of the beloved is like the spirit that moved upon the face of the waters, giving birth to heaven and earth, when the Lord spoke and said, "Let there be."

Of the First Kiss

IT IS THE FIRST SIP from the cup filled by the goddess with the nectar of Life. It is the dividing line between Doubt that beguiles the spirit and saddens the heart, and Certitude that floods the inner self with joy. It is the beginning of the song of Life and the first act in the drama of the Ideal Man. It is the bond that unites the strangeness of the past with the brightness of the future; the link between the silence of the feelings and their song. It is a word uttered by four lips proclaiming the heart a throne, Love a king, and fidelity a crown. It is the gentle touch of the delicate fingers of the breeze on the lips of the rose—uttering a long sigh of relief and a sweet moan.

It is the beginning of that magic vibration that carries the lovers from the world of weights and measures into the world of dreams and revelations.

It is the union of two fragrant flowers; and the mingling of their fragrance toward the creation of a third soul.

As the first glance is like a seed sown by the goddess in the field of the human heart, so the first kiss is the first flower at the tip of the branch of the Tree of Life.

Of Marriage

HERE LOVE BEGINS to render the prose of Life into hymns and canticles of praise, with music that is set by night, to

49

be sung in the day. Here Love's longing draws back the veil, and illumines the recesses of the heart, creating a happiness that no other happiness can surpass but that of the Soul when she embraces God.

Marriage is the union of two divinities that a third might be born on earth. It is the union of two souls in a strong love for the abolishment of separateness. It is that higher unity which fuses the separate unities within the two spirits. It is the golden ring in a chain whose beginning is a glance, and whose ending is Eternity. It is the pure rain that falls from an unblemished sky to fructify and bless the fields of divine Nature.

As the first glance from the eyes of the beloved is like a seed sown in the human heart, and the first kiss of her lips like a flower upon the branch of the Tree of Life, so the union of two lovers in marriage is like the first fruit of the first flower of that seed.

5

Of the Divinity of Man

SPRING CAME, and Nature began speaking in the murmur of brooks and rivulets and in the smiles of the flowers; and the soul of Man was made happy and content.

Then suddenly Nature waxed furious and laid waste the beautiful city. And man forgot her laughter, her sweetness, and her kindness.

In one hour a frightful, blind force had destroyed what it had taken generations to build. Terrifying death seized man and beast in his claws and crushed them.

Ravaging fires consumed man and his goods; a deep and terrifying night hid the beauty of life under a shroud of ashes. The fearful elements raged and destroyed man, his habitations, and all his handiwork.

Amidst this frightful thunder of Destruction from the bowels of the Earth, amidst all this misery and ruin, stood the poor Soul, gazing upon all this from a distance, and meditating sorrowfully upon the weakness of Man and the omnipotence of God. She reflected upon the enemy of Man hidden deep beneath the layers of the earth and among the atoms of the ether. She heard the wailing of the mothers and of the hungry children and she shared their suffering. She pondered the savagery of the elements and the smallness of Man. And she recalled how only yesterday the children of Man had slept safely in their homes—but today they were homeless fugitives, bewailing their beautiful city as they gazed upon it from a distance, their hope turned to despair, their joy to sorrow, their life of peace to warfare. She suffered with the brokenhearted, who were caught in the iron claws of Sorrow, Pain, and Despair.

And as the Soul stood there pondering, suffering, doubting the justice of the Divine Law that binds all of the world's forces, she whispered into the ear of Silence:

"Behind all this creation there is eternal Wisdom that brings forth wrath and destruction, but which will yet bring forth unpredictable beauty.

"For fire, thunder, and tempests are to the Earth what hatred, envy and evil are to the human heart. While the afflicted nation was filling the firmament with groans and lamentations, Memory brought to my mind all the warnings and calamities and tragedies that have been enacted on the stage of Time.

"I saw Man, throughout history, erecting towers, palaces, cities, temples on the face of the earth; and I saw the earth turn in her fury upon them and snatch them back into her bosom.

"I saw strong men building impregnable castles and I observed artists embellishing their walls with paintings; then I saw the earth gape, open wide her mouth, and swallow all that the skilful hand and the luminous mind of genius had shaped.

"And I knew that the earth is like a beautiful bride who needs no man-made jewels to heighten her loveliness but is content with the green verdure of her fields, and the golden sands of her seashores, and the precious stones on her mountains.

"But man in his Divinity I saw standing like a giant in the midst of Wrath and Destruction, mocking the anger of the earth and the raging of the elements.

"Like a pillar of light Man stood amidst the ruins of Babylon, Nineveh, Palmyra and Pompeii, and as he stood he sang the song of Immortality:

> *Let the Earth take*
> *That which is hers,*
> *For I, Man, have no ending.*"

6

Of Reason and Knowledge

WHEN REASON SPEAKS TO YOU, hearken to what she says, and you shall be saved. Make good use of her utterances, and you shall be as one armed. For the Lord has given you no better guide than Reason, no stronger arm than Reason. When Reason speaks to your inmost self, you are proof against Desire. For Reason is a prudent minister, a loyal guide, and a wise counsellor. Reason is light in darkness, as anger is darkness amidst light. Be wise—let Reason, not Impulse, be your guide.

Yet be mindful that even if Reason be at your side, she is helpless without the aid of Knowledge. Without her blood-sister, Knowledge, Reason is like houseless poverty; and Knowledge without Reason is like a house unguarded. And even Love, Justice, and Goodness avail little if Reason be not there too.

The learned man who has not judgment is like an un-armed soldier proceeding into battle. His wrath will poison the pure spring of the life of his community and he will be like the grain of aloes in a pitcher of pure water.

Reason and learning are like body and soul. Without the body, the soul is nothing but empty wind. Without the soul, the body is but a senseless frame.

Reason without learning is like the untilled soil, or like the human body that lacks nourishment.

Reason is not like the goods sold in the market places— the more plentiful they are, the less they are worth. Reason's worth waxes with her abundance. But were she sold in the market, it is only the wise man who would understand her true value.

The fool sees naught but folly; and the madman only madness. Yesterday I asked a foolish man to count the fools among us. He laughed and said, "This is too hard a thing to do, and it will take too long. Were it not better to count only the wise?"

Know your own true worth, and you shall not perish. Reason is your light and your beacon of Truth. Reason is the source of Life. God has given you Knowledge, so that by its light you may not only worship him, but also see yourself in your weakness and strength.

If you do not descry the mote in your own eye, surely you will not see it in your neighbor's.

Each day look into your conscience and amend your faults; if you fail in this duty you will be untrue to the Knowledge and Reason that are within you.

Keep a watchful eye over yourself as if you were your own enemy; for you cannot learn to govern yourself, unless you first learn to govern your own passions and obey the dictates of your conscience.

I once heard a learned man say, "Every evil has its remedy, except folly. To reprimand an obstinate fool or to preach to a dolt is like writing upon the water. Christ healed the blind, the halt, the palsied, and the leprous. But the fool He could not cure.

"Study a question from all sides, and you will be sure to discover where error has crept in.

"When the portal of your house is wide, see to it that the postern-gate be not too narrow.

"He who tries to seize an opportunity after it has passed him by is like one who sees it approach but will not go to meet it."

God does not work evil. He gives us Reason and Learning so that we may ever be on our guard against the pitfalls of Error and Destruction.

Blessed are they on whom God has conferred the gift of Reason.

56

7

Of Music

I SAT BY ONE whom my heart loves, and I listened to her words. My soul began to wander in the infinite spaces where the universe appeared like a dream, and the body like a narrow prison.

The enchanting voice of my Beloved entered my heart.

This is Music, oh friends, for I heard her through the sighs of the one I loved, and through the words, half-uttered between her lips.

With the eyes of my hearing I saw my Beloved's heart.

My friends: Music is the language of spirits. Its melody is like the frolicsome breeze that makes the strings quiver with love. When the gentle fingers of Music knock at the door of our feelings, they awaken memories that have long lain hidden in the depths of the Past. The sad strains of Music bring us mournful recollections; and her quiet strains bring us joyful memories. The sound of strings makes us weep at the departure of a dear one, or makes us smile at the peace God has bestowed upon us.

The soul of Music is of the Spirit, and her mind is of the Heart.

When God created Man, he gave him Music as a language different from all other languages. And early man sang her glory in the wilderness; and she drew the hearts of kings and moved them from their thrones.

Our souls are like tender flowers at the mercy of the winds of Destiny. They tremble in the morning breeze, and bend their heads under the falling dews of heaven.

The song of the bird awakens Man from his slumber, and invites him to join in the psalms of glory to Eternal Wisdom that has created the song of the bird.

Such music makes us ask ourselves the meaning of the mysteries contained in ancient books.

When the birds sing, do they call to the flowers in the fields, or are they speaking to the trees, or are they echoing the murmur of the brooks? For Man with his understanding cannot know what the bird is saying, nor what the brook is murmuring, nor what the waves whisper when they touch the beaches slowly and gently.

Man with his understanding cannot know what the rain is saying when it falls upon the leaves of the trees or when it taps at the window panes. He cannot know what the breeze is saying to the flowers in the fields.

But the Heart of Man can feel and grasp the meaning of

these sounds that play upon his feelings. Eternal Wisdom often speaks to him in a mysterious language; Soul and Nature converse together, while Man stands speechless and bewildered.

Yet has not Man wept at the sounds? And are not his tears eloquent understanding?

Divine Music!
Daughter of the Soul of Love

Vase of bitterness and of
Love

Dream of the human heart, fruit
of sorrow

Flower of joy, fragrance and
bloom of feeling

Tongue of lovers, revealer of
secrets

Mother of the tears of hidden love

Inspirer of poets, composers,
architects

Unity of thoughts within fragments
of words

59

Designer of love out of beauty
Wine of the exulting heart in
a world of dreams

Heartener of warriors, and strengthener
of souls
Ocean of mercy and sea of tenderness

O Music
In your depths we deposit our hearts
and souls
Thou hast taught us to see with our
ears
And hear with our hearts.

8

Of Wisdom

THE WISE MAN is he who loves and reveres God. A man's merit lies in his knowledge and in his deeds, not in his color, faith, race, or descent. For remember, my friend, the son of a shepherd who possesses knowledge is of greater worth to a nation than the heir to the throne, if he be ignorant. Knowledge is your true patent of nobility, no matter who your father or what your race may be.

Learning is the only wealth tyrants cannot despoil. Only death can dim the lamp of knowledge that is within you. The true wealth of a nation lies not in its gold or silver but in its learning, wisdom, and in the uprightness of its sons.

The riches of the spirit beautify the face of man and

give birth to sympathy and respect. The spirit in every being is made manifest in the eyes, the countenance, and in all bodily movements and gestures. Our appearance, our words, our actions are never greater than ourselves. For the soul is our house; our eyes its windows; and our words its messengers.

Knowledge and understanding are life's faithful companions who will never prove untrue to you. For knowledge is your crown, and understanding your staff; and when they are with you, you can possess no greater treasures.

He who understands you is greater kin to you than your own brother. For even your own kindred may neither understand you nor know your true worth.

Friendship with the ignorant is as foolish as arguing with a drunkard.

God has bestowed upon you intelligence and knowledge. Do not extinguish the lamp of Divine Grace and do not let the candle of wisdom die out in the darkness of lust and error. For a wise man approaches with his torch to light up the path of mankind.

Remember, one just man causes the Devil greater affliction than a million blind believers.

A little knowledge that *acts* is worth infinitely more than much knowledge that is idle.

If your knowledge teaches you not the value of things, and frees you not from the bondage to matter, you shall never come near the throne of Truth.

If your knowledge teaches you not to rise above human weakness and misery and lead your fellow man on the right path, you are indeed a man of little worth and will remain such till Judgment Day.

Learn the words of wisdom uttered by the wise and apply them in your own life. Live them—but do not make a show of reciting them, for he who repeats what he does not understand is no better than an ass that is loaded with books.

9

Of Love and Equality

My poor friend, if you only knew that the Poverty which causes you so much wretchedness is the very thing that reveals the knowledge of Justice and the understanding of Life, you would be contented with your lot.

I say knowledge of Justice: for the rich man is too busy amassing wealth to seek this knowledge.

And I say understanding of Life: for the strong man is too eager in his pursuit of power and glory to keep to the straight path of truth.

Rejoice then, my poor friend, for you are the mouth of Justice and the book of Life. Be content, for you are the source of virtue in those who rule over you and the pillar of integrity of those who guide you.

If you could see, my sorrowful friend, that the misfortune which has defeated you in life is the very power that illumines your heart and raises your soul from the pit of derision to the throne of reverence, you would be content with your share and you would look upon it as a legacy to instruct you and make you wise.

For Life is a chain made up of many diverse links. Sorrow is one golden link between submission to the present and the promised hope of the future.

It is the dawn between slumber and awakening.

My fellow poor, Poverty sets off the nobility of the spirit, while wealth discloses its evil. Sorrow softens the feelings, and Joy heals the wounded heart. Were Sorrow and Poverty abolished, the spirit of man would be like an empty tablet, with naught inscribed save the signs of selfishness and greed.

Remember that Divinity is the true self of Man. It cannot be sold for gold; neither can it be heaped up as are the riches of the world today. The rich man has cast off his Divinity, and has clung to his gold. And the young today have forsaken their Divinity and pursue self-indulgence and pleasure.

My beloved poor, the hour you spend with your wife and your children when you return home from the field is the earnest of all human families to come; it is the emblem of the happiness that will be the lot of all coming generations.

But the life that the rich man spends in heaping up gold is in truth like the life of the worms in the grave. It is a sign of fear.

The tears you shed, my sorrowful friend, are purer than

the laughter of him that seeks to forget and sweeter than the mockery of the scoffer. These tears cleanse the heart of the blight of hatred, and teach man to share the pain of the brokenhearted. They are the tears of the Nazarene.

The strength you sow for the rich you shall reap in time to come, for all things return to their source, according to the Law of Nature.

And the sorrow you have borne shall be turned to gladness by the will of Heaven.

And generations to come shall learn of Sorrow and Poverty a lesson of Love and Equality.

IO

Further Sayings of the Master

I HAVE BEEN HERE since the beginning, and I shall be until the end of days; for there is no ending to my existence. The human soul is but a part of a burning torch which God separated from Himself at Creation.

My brothers, seek counsel of one another, for therein lies the way out of error and futile repentance. The wisdom of the many is your shield against tyranny. For when we turn to one another for counsel we reduce the number of our enemies.

He who does not seek advice is a fool. His folly blinds him to Truth and makes him evil, stubborn, and a danger to his fellow man.

When you have grasped a problem clearly, face it with resolution, for that is the way of the strong.

Seek ye counsel of the aged, for their eyes have looked on the faces of the years and their ears have hearkened to the voices of Life. Even if their counsel is displeasing to you, pay heed to them.

Do not expect good counsel from a tyrant, or a wrongdoer, or a presumptuous man, or a deserter from honor. Woe to him who conspires with the wrongdoer who comes seeking advice. For to agree with the wrongdoer is infamy, and to hearken to that which is false is treachery.

Unless I be endowed with wide knowledge, keen judgment and great experience, I cannot account myself a counsellor of men.

Make haste slowly, and do not be slothful when opportunity beckons. Thus you will avoid grave errors.

My friend, be not like him who sits by his fireside and watches the fire go out, then blows vainly upon the dead ashes. Do not give up hope or yield to despair because of that which is past, for to bewail the irretrievable is the worst of human frailties.

Yesterday I repented of my deed, and today I understand my error and the evil I brought upon myself when I broke my bow and destroyed my quiver.

68

I love you, my brother, whoever you are—whether you worship in your church, kneel in your temple, or pray in your mosque. You and I are all children of one faith, for the divers paths of religion are fingers of the loving hand of one Supreme Being, a hand extended to all, offering completeness of spirit to all, eager to receive all.

God has given you a spirit with wings on which to soar into the spacious firmament of Love and Freedom. Is it not pitiful then that you cut your wings with your own hands and suffer your soul to crawl like an insect upon the earth?

My soul, living is like a courser of the night; the swifter its flight, the nearer the dawn.

I I

The Listener

OH WIND, you who pass by us, now singing sweetly and softly, now sighing and lamenting: we hear you, but we cannot see you. We feel your touch, but we cannot descry your shape. You are like an ocean of love that engulfs our spirits, but does not drown them.

You ascend with the hills, and descend with the valleys, diffusing yourself over field and meadow. There is strength in your ascent and gentleness in your descent; and grace in your dispersion. You are like a merciful king, gracious toward the oppressed, but stern toward the arrogant and strong.

In Autumn you moan through the valleys, and the trees echo your wailing. In Winter you break your chains, and all Nature rebels with you.

In Spring you stir from your slumbers, still weak and infirm, and through your faint stirrings the fields begin to awake.

In Summer you hide behind the veil of Silence as if you had died, smitten by the shafts of the sun and the spears of heat.

Were you indeed lamenting in the late Autumn days, or were you laughing at the blushes of the naked trees? Were you angry in Winter, or were you dancing around the snow-decked tomb of Night?

Were you indeed languishing in the Spring, or were you grieving for the loss of your beloved, the Youth of all Seasons?

Were you perchance dead in those Summer days, or were you only asleep in the heart of the fruits, in the eyes of the vineyards, or in the ears of the wheat upon the threshing floors?

From the streets of the cities you raise up and bear the seeds of plagues; and from the hills you waft the fragrant breath of flowers. Thus the great Soul sustains the sorrow of Life and silently meets its joys.

Into the ears of the rose you whisper a secret whose meaning she grasps: often she is troubled—then she rejoices. Such is the way of God with the soul of Man.

Now you tarry. Now you hasten here and yonder, moving ceaselessly. Such too is the mind of Man, who lives when he acts and dies when he is idle.

You write your songs on the face of the waters; then you erase them. So does the poet when he is creating.

From the South you come as warm as Love; and from the North as cold as Death. From the East as gentle as the touch of the Soul; and from the West as fierce as Wrath and Fury. Are you as fickle as Age, or are you the courier of weighty tidings from the four points of the compass?

You rage through the desert, you trample the innocent caravans underfoot and bury them in mountains of sand. Are you that same frolicsome breeze that trembles with the dawn among the leaves and branches and flits like a dream through the windings of the valleys where the flowers bow in greeting and where the grass droops heavy-lidded with the intoxication of your breath?

You rise from the oceans and shake their silent depths from your tresses, and in your rage you lay waste ships and crews. Are you that selfsame gentle breeze that caresses the locks of children as they play around their homes?

Whither do you carry our hearts, our sighs, our breaths, our smiles? What do you do with the flying torches of our souls? Do you bear them beyond the horizon of Life? Do you drag them like sacrificial victims to distant and horrible caves to destroy them?

In the still night, hearts reveal their secrets to you. And at dawn, eyes open at your gentle touch. Are you mindful of what the heart has felt or the eyes have seen?

Between your wings the anguished lays the echo of his mournful songs, the orphan the fragments of his broken heart, and the oppressed his painful sighs. Within the folds of your mantle the stranger lays his longing, the forsaken his burden, and the fallen woman her despair.

Do you preserve all these in safekeeping for the humble?

Or are you like Mother Earth, who entombs all that she brings forth?

Do you hear these cries and lamentations? Do you hear these moans and sighs? Or are you like the proud and mighty who do not see the outstretched hand or hear the cries of the poor?

O Life of all Listeners, do you hear?

I2

Love and Youth

A YOUTH IN THE DAWN OF LIFE sat at his desk in a solitary house. Now he looked through the window at the sky that was studded with glittering stars, now he turned his gaze toward a maiden's picture, which he held in his hand. Its lines and colors were worthy of a master; they became reflected in the youth's mind, and opened to him the secrets of the World and the mystery of Eternity.

The picture of the woman called to the youth, and at that moment turned his eyes into ears, so that he understood the language of the spirits that hovered over the room, and his heart became seared with love.

Thus the hours passed as if they were only a moment of some beautiful dream, or only a year in a life of Eternity.

Then the youth set the picture before him, took up his pen, and poured out his heart's feelings upon the parchment:

"Beloved: Great truth that transcends Nature does not pass from one being to another by way of human speech. Truth chooses Silence to convey her meaning to loving souls.

"I know that the silence of the night is the worthiest messenger between our two hearts, for she bears Love's message and recites the psalms of our hearts. Just as God has made our souls prisoners of our bodies, so Love has made me a prisoner of words and speech.

"They say, O Beloved, that Love is a devouring flame in the heart of man. I knew at our first meeting that I had known you for ages, and I knew at the time of parting that nothing was strong enough to keep us apart.

"My first glimpse of you was not in truth the first. The hour in which our hearts met confirmed in me the belief in Eternity and in the immortality of the Soul.

"At such a moment Nature lifts the veil from him who believes himself oppressed, and reveals her everlasting justice.

"Do you recall the brook by which we sat and gazed at each other, Beloved? Do you know your eyes told me at that moment that your love was not born of pity but of justice? And now I can proclaim to myself and to the world that the gifts which derive from justice are greater than those that spring from charity.

"And I can say too that Love which is the child of chance is like the stagnant waters of the marshes.

"Beloved, before me stretches a life which I can fashion

75

into greatness and beauty—a life that began with our first meeting, and which will last to eternity.

"For I know that it is within you to bring forth the power that God has bestowed upon me, to be embodied in great words and deeds, even as the sun brings to life the fragrant flowers of the field.

"And thus, my love for you shall endure for ever."

The youth rose and walked slowly and reverently across the room. He looked through the window and saw the moon rising above the horizon and filling the spacious sky with her gentle radiance.

Then he returned to his desk and wrote:

"Forgive me, my Beloved, for speaking to you in the second person. For you are my other, beautiful, half, which I have lacked ever since we emerged from the sacred hand of God. Forgive me, my Beloved!"

13

Wisdom and I

IN THE SILENCE OF THE NIGHT, Wisdom came into my chamber and stood by my bed. She gazed upon me like a loving mother, dried my tears, and said:

"I have heard the cries of your soul, and have come here to comfort you. Open your heart to me and I shall fill it with light. Ask, and I shall show you the path of Truth."

I complied with her bidding, and asked:

"Who am I, Wisdom, and how came I to this place of horrors? What are these mighty hopes, these mountains of books, and these strange figures? What are these thoughts that come and go like a flock of doves? What are these words we compose with desire and write down in joy? What are these sorrowful and joyous conclusions that embrace my soul and envelope my heart? Whose are these eyes that stare at me and pierce the very inmost recesses of my soul, and yet are oblivious of my grief? What are these voices that lament the passing of my days and chant the praises of my childhood? Who is this youth that toys with my desires and mocks my feelings, forgetting the deeds of yesterday, contenting himself with the littleness of today, and arming himself against the slow approach of tomorrow?

"What is this dreadful world that moves me and to what unknown land?

"What is this earth that opens wide her jaws to swallow our bodies and prepares an everlasting shelter for greed? Who is this Man who contents himself with the favors of Fortune and craves a kiss from the lips of Life while Death smites him in the face? Who is this Man who buys a moment of pleasure with a year of repentance and gives himself over to sleep, while dreams call to him? Who is this Man who swims on the waves of Ignorance toward the gulf of Darkness?

"Tell me, Wisdom, what are all these things?"

And Wisdom opened her lips and spoke:

"You, Man, would see the world with the eyes of God, and would grasp the secrets of the hereafter by means of human thought. Such is the fruit of ignorance.

"Go into the field, and see how the bee hovers over the sweet flowers and the eagle swoops down on its prey. Go into your neighbor's house and see the infant child bewitched by the firelight, while the mother is busied at her tasks. Be like the bee, and do not waste your spring days gazing on the doings of the eagle. Be like the child rejoicing at the firelight and let the mother be. All that you see was, and still is, yours.

"The many books and strange figures and the lovely thoughts around you are ghosts of the spirits that have been before you. The words your lips utter are the links in the chain that binds you and your fellow men. The sorrowful and joyful conclusions are the seeds sown by the past in the field of your soul to be reaped by the future.

"The youth that toys with your desires is he who will open the gate of your heart for Light to enter. The earth that opens wide her mouth to swallow man and his works is the redeemer of our souls from bondage to our bodies.

"The world that moves with you is your heart, which is the world itself. And Man, whom you deem so small and ignorant, is God's messenger who has come to learn the joy of life through sorrow and gain knowledge from ignorance."

Thus spoke Wisdom, and laid a hand upon my burning brow, saying:

"March on. Do not tarry. To go forward is to move toward perfection. March on, and fear not the thorns or the sharp stones on Life's path."

14

The Two Cities

LIFE TOOK ME UP ON HER WINGS and bore me to the top of Mount Youth. Then she beckoned and pointed behind her. I looked back and saw a strange city, from which rose dark smoke of many hues moving slowly like phantoms. A thin cloud almost hid the city from my gaze.

After a moment of silence, I exclaimed: "What is this I see, Life?"

And Life answered: "This is the City of the Past. Look upon it and ponder."

And I gazed upon this wonderful scene and I saw many objects and sights: halls built for action, standing giant-like beneath the wings of Slumber; temples of talk around which hovered spirits at once crying in despair, and singing songs of hope. I saw churches built by Faith and destroyed by Doubt. I spied minarets of Thought, lifting their spires like the upraised arms of beggars; I saw avenues of Desire stretching like rivers through valleys; storehouses of secrets guarded by sentinels of Concealment and pillaged by thieves of Disclosure; towers of strength raised by Valor and demolished by Fear; shrines of Dreams, embellished by Slumber and destroyed by Wakefulness; slight huts inhabited by Weakness; mosques of Solitude and Self-Denial; institutions of learning lighted by Intelligence and darkened by Ignorance; taverns of Love, where lovers became drunk and Emptiness mocked at them; theatres upon whose boards Life acted out its play, and Death rounded out Life's tragedies.

Such is the City of the Past—in appearance far away, though in reality nearby—visible, though barely, through the dark clouds.

Then Life beckoned to me and said, "Follow me. We have tarried here too long." And I replied, "Whither are we going, Life?"

And Life said, "We are going to the City of the Future."

And I said, "Have pity on me, Life. I am weary, and my feet are bruised and the strength is gone out of me."

But Life replied, "March on, my friend. Tarrying is cowardice. To remain forever gazing upon the City of the Past is Folly. Behold, the City of the Future beckons. . . ."

15

Nature and Man

AT DAYBREAK I sat in a field, holding converse with Nature, while Man rested peacefully under coverlets of slumber. I lay in the green grass and meditated upon these questions: "Is Truth Beauty? Is Beauty Truth?"

And in my thoughts I found myself carried far from mankind, and my imagination lifted the veil of matter that hid my inner self. My soul expanded and I was brought closer to Nature and her secrets, and my ears were opened to the language of her wonders.

As I sat thus deep in thought, I felt a breeze passing through the branches of the trees, and I heard a sighing like that of a strayed orphan.

"Why do you sigh, gentle breeze?" I asked.

And the breeze replied, "Because I have come from the city that is aglow with the heat of the sun, and the seeds of plagues and contaminations cling to my pure garments. Can you blame me for grieving?"

Then I looked at the tear-stained faces of the flowers, and heard their soft lament. And I asked, "Why do you weep, my lovely flowers?"

One of the flowers raised her gentle head and whispered, "We weep because Man will come and cut us down, and offer us for sale in the markets of the city."

And another flower added, "In the evening, when we are wilted, he will throw us on the refuse heap. We weep because the cruel hand of Man snatches us from our native haunts."

And I heard the brook lamenting like a widow mourning her dead child and I asked, "Why do you weep, my pure brook?"

And the brook replied, "Because I am compelled to go to the city where Man contemns me and spurns me for stronger drinks and makes of me a scavenger for his offal, pollutes my purity, and turns my goodness to filth."

And I heard the birds grieving, and I asked, "Why do you cry, my beautiful birds?" And one of them flew near, and perched at the tip of a branch and said, "The sons of Adam will soon come into this field with their deadly weapons and make war upon us as if we were their mortal enemies. We are now taking leave of one another, for we know not which of us will escape the wrath of Man. Death follows us wherever we go."

Now the sun rose from behind the mountain peaks, and gilded the treetops with coronals. I looked upon this beauty and asked myself, "Why must Man destroy what Nature has built?"

16

The Enchantress

THE WOMAN WHOM MY HEART HAS LOVED sat yesterday in this lonely room and rested her lovely body upon this velvet couch. From these crystal goblets she sipped the aged wine.

This is yesterday's dream; for the woman my heart has loved is gone to a distant place—the Land of Oblivion and Emptiness.

The print of her fingers is yet upon my mirror; and the fragrance of her breathing is still within the folds of my garments; and the echo of her sweet voice can be heard in this room.

But the woman my heart has loved is gone to a distant place called the Valley of Exile and Forgetfulness.

By my bed hangs a portrait of this woman. The love-letters she wrote to me I have kept in a silver case, studded with emeralds and coral. And all these things will remain with me till tomorrow, when the wind will blow them away into oblivion, where only mute silence reigns.

The woman I have loved is like the women to whom you have given your hearts. She is strangely beautiful, as if fashioned by a god; as meek as the dove, as wily as the serpent, as proudly graceful as the peacock, as fierce as the wolf, as lovely as the white swan, and as fearful as the black night. She is compounded of a handful of earth and a beakerful of sea-foam.

I have known this woman since childhood. I have followed her into the fields and laid hold of the hem of her garments as she walked in the streets of the city. I have known her since the days of my youth, and I have seen the shadow of her face in the pages of the books I have read. I have heard her heavenly voice in the murmur of the brook.

To her I opened my heart's discontents and the secrets of my soul.

The woman whom my heart has loved is gone to a cold, desolate and distant place—the Land of Emptiness and Oblivion.

The woman my heart has loved is called *Life*. She is beautiful, and draws all hearts to herself. She takes our lives in pawn and buries our yearnings in promises.

Life is a woman bathing in the tears of her lovers and anointing herself with the blood of her victims. Her raiments are white days, lined with the darkness of night. She takes the human heart to lover, but denies herself in marriage.

> *Life is an enchantress*
> *Who seduces us with her beauty—*
> *But he who knows her wiles*
> *Will flee her enchantments.*

17

Youth and Hope

YOUTH WALKED BEFORE ME and I followed him until we came to a distant field. There he stopped, and gazed at the clouds that drifted over the horizon like a flock of white lambs. Then he looked at the trees whose naked branches pointed toward the sky as if praying to Heaven for the return of their foliage.

And I said, "Where are we now, Youth?"

And he replied, "We are in the field of Bewilderment. Take heed."

And I said, "Let us go back at once, for this desolate place affrights me, and the sight of the clouds and the naked trees saddens my heart."

And he replied, "Be patient. Perplexity is the beginning of knowledge."

Then I looked around me and saw a form moving gracefully toward us and I asked, "Who is this woman?"

And Youth replied, "This is Melpomene, daughter of Zeus, and Muse of Tragedy."

"Oh, happy Youth!" I exclaimed, "what does Tragedy want of me, while you are at my side?"

And he answered, "She has come to show you the earth and its sorrows; for he who has not looked on Sorrow will never see Joy."

Then the spirit laid a hand upon my eyes. When she withdrew it, Youth was gone, and I was alone, divested of my earthly garments, and I cried, "Daughter of Zeus, where is Youth?"

Melpomene did not answer; but took me up under her wings, and carried me to the summit of a high mountain. Below me I saw the earth and all in it, spread out like the pages of a book, upon which were inscribed the secrets of the universe. I stood in awe beside the maiden, pondered the mystery of Man, and struggled to decipher Life's symbols.

And I saw woeful things: The Angels of Happiness warring with the Devils of Misery, and standing between them was Man, now drawn one way by Hope and now another by Despair.

I saw Love and Hate dallying with the human heart; Love concealing Man's guilt and besotting him with the wine of submission, praise and flattery; while Hatred provoked him, and sealed his ears and blinded his eyes to Truth.

And I beheld the city crouching like a child of its slums and snatching at the garment of the son of Adam. From afar I saw the lovely fields weeping over man's sorrow.

I beheld priests foaming like sly foxes; and false messiahs contriving and conspiring against Man's happiness.

And I saw Man calling upon Wisdom for deliverance; but Wisdom did not hearken to his cries, for he had contemned her when she spoke to him in the streets of the city.

And I saw preachers gazing in adoration toward the heavens, while their hearts were interred in the pits of Greed.

I saw a youth winning a maiden's heart with sweet speech; but their true feelings were asleep, and their divinity was far away.

I saw the lawmakers chattering idly, selling their wares in the market places of Deceit and Hypocrisy.

I saw physicians toying with the souls of the simple-hearted and trustful. I saw the ignorant sitting with the wise, exalting their past to the throne of glory, adorning their present with the robes of plenty, and preparing a couch of luxury for the future.

I saw the wretched poor sowing the seed, and the strong reaping; and oppression, miscalled Law, standing guard.

I saw the thieves of Ignorance despoiling the treasures of Knowledge, while the sentinels of Light lay drowned in the deep sleep of inaction.

And I saw two lovers; but the woman was like a lute in the hand of a man who cannot play, but understands only harsh sounds.

And I beheld the forces of Knowledge laying siege to the

city of Inherited Privilege; but they were few in number and were soon dispersed.

And I saw Freedom walking alone, knocking at doors, and asking for shelter, but no one heeded her pleas. Then I saw Prodigality striding in splendor, and the multitude acclaiming her as Liberty.

I saw Religion buried in books, and Doubt stood in her place.

And I saw Man wearing the garments of Patience as a cloak for Cowardice and calling Sloth Tolerance, and Fear Courtesy.

I saw the intruder sitting at the board of Knowledge, uttering folly, but the guests were silent.

I saw gold in the hands of the wasteful, a means of evil-doing; and in the hands of the miserly as a bait for hatred. But in the hands of the wise I saw no gold.

When I beheld all these things, I cried out in pain, "Oh Daughter of Zeus, is this indeed the Earth? Is this Man?"

In a soft and anguished voice she replied, "What you see is the Soul's path, and it is paved with sharp stones and carpeted with thorns. This is only the shadow of Man. This is Night. But wait! Morning will soon be here!"

Then she laid a gentle hand upon my eyes, and when she withdrew it, behold! there was Youth walking slowly by my side, and ahead of us, leading the way, marched Hope.

18

Resurrection

YESTERDAY, MY BELOVED, I was almost alone in the world, and my solitude was as pitiless as death. I was like a flower that grows in the shadow of a huge rock, of whose existence Life is not aware, and which is not aware of Life.

But today my soul awakened, and I beheld you standing by my side. I rose to my feet and rejoiced; then I knelt in reverence and worshipped before you.

Yesterday the touch of the frolicsome breeze seemed harsh, my beloved, and the sun's beams seemed weak, a mist hid the face of the earth, and the waves of the ocean roared like a tempest.

I looked all about me, but saw naught but my own suffering self standing by my side, while the phantoms of darkness rose and fell around me like ravenous vultures.

But today Nature is bathed in light, and the roaring waves are calm and the fogs are dispersed. Wherever I look I see Life's secrets lying open before me.

Yesterday I was a soundless word in the heart of the Night; today I am a song on the lips of Time.

And all this has come to pass in a moment, and was fashioned by a glance, a word, a sigh, and a kiss.

That moment, my beloved, has blended my soul's past readiness with my heart's hopes of the future. It was like a white rose that bursts from the bosom of the earth into the light of day.

That moment was to my life what the birth of Christ has been to the ages of Man, for it was filled with love and goodness. It turned darkness into light, sorrow into joy, and despair to bliss.

Beloved, the fires of Love descend from heaven in many shapes and forms, but their impress on the world is one. The tiny flame that lights up the human heart is like a blazing torch that comes down from heaven to light up the paths of mankind.

For in one soul are contained the hopes and feelings of all Mankind.

The Jews, my beloved, awaited the coming of a Messiah, who had been promised them, and who was to deliver them from bondage.

And the Great Soul of the World sensed that the worship of Jupiter and Minerva no longer availed, for the thirsty hearts of men could not be quenched with that wine.

In Rome men pondered the divinity of Apollo, a god

without pity, and the beauty of Venus already fallen into decay.

For deep in their hearts, though they did not understand it, these nations hungered and thirsted for the supreme teaching that would transcend any to be found on the earth. They yearned for the spirit's freedom that would teach man to rejoice with his neighbor at the light of the sun and the wonder of living. For it is this cherished freedom that brings man close to the Unseen, which he can approach without fear or shame.

All this took place two thousand years ago, my beloved, when the heart's desires hovered around visible things, fearful of approaching the eternal spirit—while Pan, Lord of Forests, filled the hearts of shepherds with terror, and Baal, Lord of the Sun, pressed with the merciless hands of priests upon the souls of the poor and lowly.

And in one night, in one hour, in one moment of time, the lips of the spirit parted and spoke the sacred word, "Life"; and it became flesh in an infant lying asleep in the lap of a virgin, in a stable where shepherds guarded their flocks against the assault of wild beasts of the night and looked with wonder upon that humble infant, asleep in the manger.

The Infant King, swaddled in his mother's wretched garments, sat upon a throne of burdened hearts and hungry souls, and through his humility wrested the sceptre of power from the hands of Jove and gave it to the poor shepherd watching over his flock.

93

And from Minerva he took Wisdom, and set it in the heart of a poor fisherman who was mending his fishing net.

From Apollo he drew Joy through his own sorrows and bestowed it upon the brokenhearted beggar by the wayside.

From Venus he took Beauty and poured it into the soul of the fallen woman trembling before her cruel oppressor.

He dethroned Baal and set in his place the humble plowman, who sowed his seed and tilled the soil by the sweat of his brow.

Beloved, was not my soul yesterday like unto the tribes of Israel? Did I not wait in the silence of the night for the coming of my Savior to deliver me from the bondage and evils of Time? Did I not feel the great thirst and the spirit's hunger as did those nations of the past? Did I not walk the road of Life like a child lost in some wilderness, and was not my life like a seed cast upon a stone, that no bird would seek, nor the elements split and bring to life?

All this came to pass yesterday, my beloved, when my dreams crouched in the dark, and feared the approach of the day.

All this came to pass when Sorrow tore my heart, and Hope strove to mend it.

In one night, in one hour, in one moment of time, the Spirit descended from the center of the circle of divine light and looked at me with your heart's eyes. From that glance Love was born, and found a dwelling in my heart.

This great Love, swaddled in the robes of my feelings,

has turned sorrow to joy, despair to bliss, aloneness to paradise.

Love, the great King, has restored life to my dead self; returned light to my tear-blinded eyes: raised me up from the pit of despair to the celestial kingdom of Hope.

For all my days were as nights, my beloved. But behold! the dawn has come; soon the sun will rise. For the breath of the Infant Jesus has filled the firmament and is mingled with the ether. Life, once full of woe, is now overflowing with joy, for the arms of the Infant are around me and embrace my soul.

Printed in the United States
17187LVS00007B/201

9 780806 500225